P9-BYE-528

MAR 1 6

AWESOME DOGS

German Shepherds

by Chris Bowman

BLASTOFF!
2
READERS

BELLWETHER MEDIA · MINNEAPOLIS, MN

Note to Librarians, Teachers, and Parents:

Blastoff! Readers are carefully developed by literacy experts and combine standards-based content with developmentally appropriate text.

Level 1 provides the most support through repetition of high-frequency words, light text, predictable sentence patterns, and strong visual support.

Level 2 offers early readers a bit more challenge through varied simple sentences, increased text load, and less repetition of high-frequency words.

Level 3 advances early-fluent readers toward fluency through increased text and concept load, less reliance on visuals, longer sentences, and more literary language.

Level 4 builds reading stamina by providing more text per page, increased use of punctuation, greater variation in sentence patterns, and increasingly challenging vocabulary.

Level 5 encourages children to move from "learning to read" to "reading to learn" by providing even more text, varied writing styles, and less familiar topics.

Whichever book is right for your reader, Blastoff! Readers are the perfect books to build confidence and encourage a love of reading that will last a lifetime!

This edition first published in 2016 by Bellwether Media, Inc.

No part of this publication may be reproduced in whole or in part without written permission of the publisher. For information regarding permission, write to Bellwether Media, Inc., Attention: Permissions Department, 5357 Penn Avenue South, Minneapolis, MN 55419.

Library of Congress Cataloging-in-Publication Data

Bowman, Chris, 1990- author.
  German Shepherds / by Chris Bowman.
    pages cm. – (Blastoff! Readers. Awesome Dogs)
  Summary: "Relevant images match informative text in this introduction to German shepherds. Intended for students in kindergarten through third grade"– Provided by publisher.
  Audience: Ages 5-8
  Audience: K to grade 3
  Includes bibliographical references and index.
  ISBN 978-1-62617-240-1 (hardcover: alk. paper)
  1. German shepherd dog–Juvenile literature. I. Title.
  SF429.G37B686 2016
  636.737'6–dc23
                        2015006565

Printed in the United States of America, North Mankato, MN.

Table of Contents

What Are German Shepherds?   4

History of German Shepherds   12

Smart Workers   16

Glossary   22

To Learn More   23

Index   24

What Are German Shepherds?

German shepherds are strong and smart dogs.

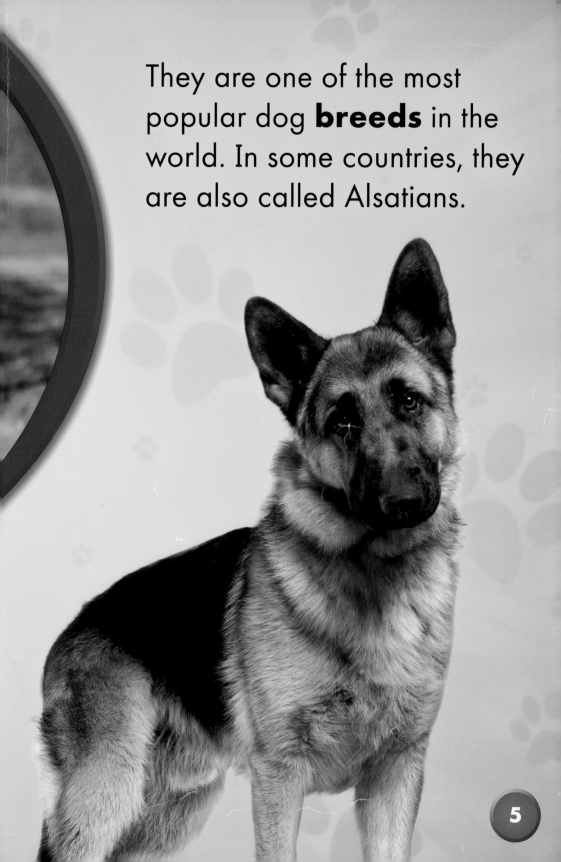

They are one of the most popular dog **breeds** in the world. In some countries, they are also called Alsatians.

5

German shepherds are large dogs with long bodies. They have pointed ears and dark eyes.

Their tails are long and **bushy**.

A German shepherd has two **coats**. The outer coat has thick, straight fur.

The **undercoat** is soft and **dense**. Shorter fur covers the head and legs.

Many colors make up a
German shepherd's coat.

German Shepherd Coats

black   brown   white

Colors include black, tan, red, and brown. Some dogs are mostly gray or white.

Max von
Stephanitz

In 1898, a German captain
named Max von Stephanitz
had a goal.

He wanted the best herding
dog in the world.

Germany

N
W E
S

He found a dog that was smart and **athletic**. Then he **bred** it with other herding dogs to make German shepherds.

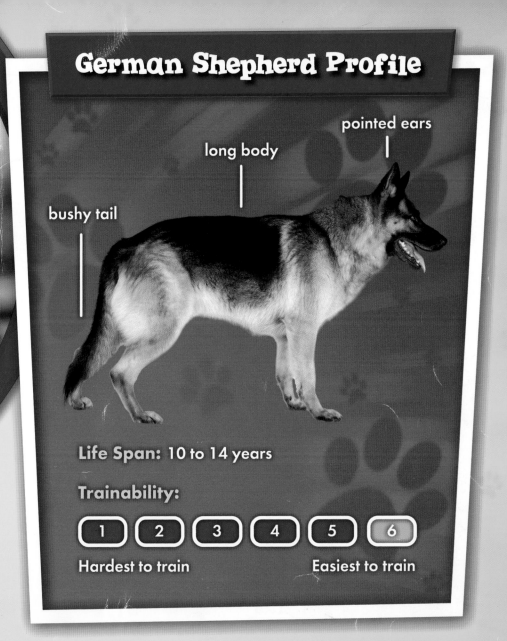

German Shepherd Profile

pointed ears

long body

bushy tail

Life Span: 10 to 14 years

Trainability:

1   2   3   4   5   6

Hardest to train   Easiest to train

Today, the **American Kennel Club** places these dogs in the **Herding Group**.

German shepherds are quick learners. They are good at following directions.

This makes them great **service dogs**. Some work with **search and rescue**.

Many German shepherds work for the police and military.

They sniff for illegal drugs or weapons.

German shepherds also make **loyal** pets.

These dogs are a perfect fit for active families. They have a lot of energy!

Glossary

American Kennel Club—an organization that keeps track of dog breeds in the United States

athletic—being strong, fit, and active

bred—purposely mated two dogs to make puppies with certain qualities

breeds—types of dogs

bushy—thick and full

coats—the hair or fur covering some animals

dense—close together

Herding Group—a group of dog breeds that like to control the movement of other animals

loyal—having constant support for someone

search and rescue—teams that look for and help people in danger

service dogs—dogs trained to help people who have special needs perform daily tasks

undercoat—a layer of short, soft hair or fur some dog breeds have to keep warm

To Learn More

AT THE LIBRARY
Barnes, Nico. *German Shepherds*. Minneapolis, Minn.: Abdo Kids, 2014.

Bodden, Valerie. *German Shepherds*. Mankato, Minn.: Creative Education, 2014.

Shores, Erika L. *All About German Shepherds*. North Mankato, Minn.: Capstone Press, 2013.

ON THE WEB
Learning more about German shepherds is as easy as 1, 2, 3.

1. Go to www.factsurfer.com.

2. Enter "German shepherds" into the search box.

3. Click the "Surf" button and you will see a list of related web sites.

With factsurfer.com, finding more information is just a click away.

Index

American Kennel Club, 15

bodies, 6, 15

bred, 14

breeds, 5

coats, 8, 9, 10, 11

colors, 10, 11

ears, 6, 15

energy, 21

eyes, 6

families, 21

fur, 8, 9

Germany, 12, 13

head, 9

herding, 13, 14

Herding Group, 15

intelligence, 4, 14, 16

legs, 9

life span, 15

names, 5

pets, 20

search and rescue, 17

service dogs, 17

size, 6

tails, 7, 15

trainability, 15, 16

undercoat, 9

von Stephanitz, Max (captain), 12

work, 17, 18

The images in this book are reproduced through the courtesy of: Eric Isselee, front cover, pp. 5, 11 (left, center, right); Gerard Lacz/ SuperStock, p. 4; photovova, p. 6; Rita Kochmarjova, pp. 7, 14; VKarlov, p. 8; Jennay Hitesman, p. 9; Nikolai Tsvetkov, pp. 10-11; Wikipedia, p. 12; purplequeue, pp. 13, 15; AnetaPics, p. 16; Christian Arnal/ Photononstop/ Glow Images, p. 17; Nancy Nehring, p. 18; imagebroker/ SuperStock, p. 19; Marc Romanelli/ Glow Images, p. 20; Juniors Bildarchiv/ Glow Images, p. 21.